A Complete Guide to Breeding

Stick and Leaf Insects

Paul D Brock

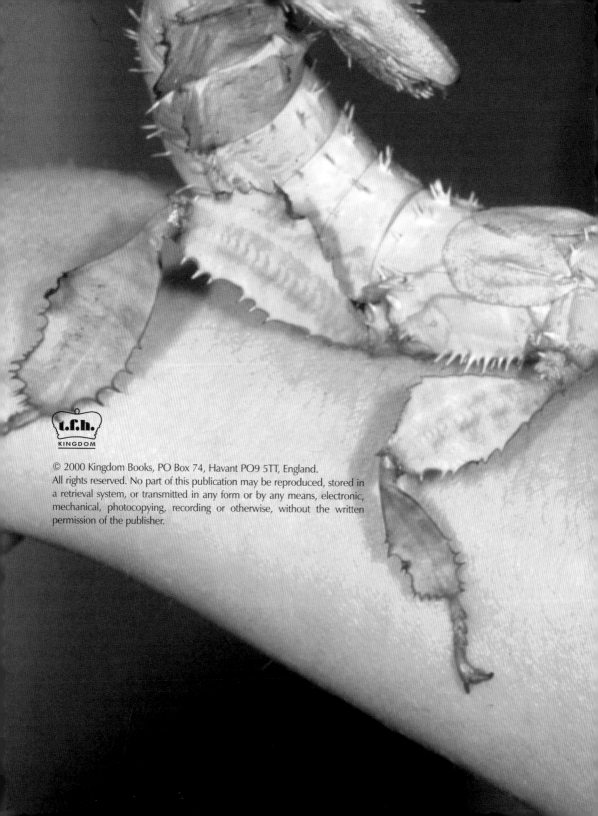

© 2000 Kingdom Books, PO Box 74, Havant PO9 5TT, England.

contents

Photographs by:
Paul D Brock (Slough, Berkshire, United Kingdom)/Christoph Seiler (Altlussheim, Germany)/
Steve Wilson (Cedar Creek, Queensland, Australia)
Watercolours of Macleay's Spectre by:
Felicity Cole (Stoke Bliss, Near Tenbury Wells, Worcestershire, United Kingdom)
Front cover: Giant Spiny Stick Insect (female)   Back cover: Javan Leaf Insect (female)

Introduction

Macleay's Spectre female: uncommon green colour form of this popular species.

Stick and leaf insects are fascinating insects. Where else could you find small to giant insects as pets, observe strange behaviour, keep spiny monsters or vividly coloured winged insects, placid twigs or broad leaf-like creatures! An excellent choice of different species is available to pet owners, who can purchase or make suitable cages for them, and purchase or obtain insects free of charge. For those on a low budget, there are few better pets to keep; even maintenance is minimal, as the insects need to be cleaned out only once a week, or sooner if the food-plant leaves become dried up. Those who like to be self-sufficient may even grow food for them in their own gardens. Keepers of stick insects include zoos, butterfly houses and individuals of all ages. Rearers are often amateur (or occasionally professional) entomologists (people who study and collect insects), who may keep other live insects.

This book will take you through the basics and also elaborate on the more advanced techniques of breeding stick and leaf insects (often called 'phasmids'). Advanced studies on classification and collecting phasmids in the wild have already been published elsewhere and references are provided for those wishing to expand their knowledge. The choice of what stage of insects to obtain, or indeed which species, is a personal decision but suggestions are offered to help you decide, along with a trouble-shooter section if you encounter serious problems. The species readily available in culture are discussed in detail, with brief notes on some other species. Who knows, you may end up joining an organisation dedicated to the study of phasmids and keep these insects for many years to come.

Common names of phasmids are referred to, where these have been designated. Scientific names are also given. These always consist of two parts - the first indicating the genus and the second the species. A genus is a collection of allied species. Each kind of phasmid is described as a species.

Female of *Clonopsis gallica* on broom in the Algarve, Portugal.

Twelve Facts About Phasmids *one*

1   Stick and leaf insects (phasmids) belong to the insect order Phasmida, also variably known as Phasmatodea, Phasmatoptera, Cheleutoptera and others, because authors cannot even agree on the name. Phasmida is the earliest (and simplest) name proposed for this order: *Phasma* is Greek for 'spectre', 'apparition' or 'phantom', relating to the phasmid's ghost-like ability to blend in with its background.

2   There are about 2500 species of phasmid, of which only about 30 are true leaf insects. They are often abundant in the tropics, although there are relatively few species in temperate regions. All feed on plants, of which bramble leaves are often successfully used as a substitute food plant in captivity, irrespective of what plants are available in the wild. The classification of phasmids is complex, with many errors in the literature. They are understudied insects and a walk in rainforests may even produce an undescribed insect.

3   In the 1700–1800s, the common name of phasmids ranged from Spectres to Phantoms, Devil's Horses, Soldiers of Cayenne, Animated Sticks, Prairie Alligators, Stick Bugs, Witch's Horses, Devil's Darning Needles, Scorpions, Dragons and others. Stick insects are known as Walkingsticks in the United States of America.

4   The original female specimen of the stick insect *Phobaeticus kirbyi* from Borneo (found in Kalimantan, Sarawak and Sabah, and also found in Brunei), was 328mm (13in) from her head to the end of her abdomen, and 546mm (21.5in) including outstretched legs, which fully justifies the title of 'longest insect in the world'. In terms of overall length, females of the closely related *Phobaeticus serratipes* from the Malay Peninsula can be longer – up to 555mm (22in), although they have a shorter body length of 278mm (11in). Both species were recently transferred to a new genus *Baculolonga*, although there are doubts whether this is a valid name.

Timema cristinae pair, with the smaller male mounted on the female.

The longest known male stick insect is the recently described *Phobaeticus heusii* from Vietnam at 250.5mm (10in), which could easily take the title of longest insect if large females are found. So far these have only been recorded up to 293mm (11.5in). The smallest stick insect is the male of *Timema cristinae* from California, United States of America, at 11.6mm (0.5in).

The longest leaf insect *Phyllium giganteum* (from the Malay Peninsula and Sarawak), reaches 113mm (4.5in), and even the male at 81mm (3in) is longer than many other female leaf insect species.

5 Each female lays 100 or more eggs, which often resemble seeds. Studies of females of *Acrophylla titan* from Deception Bay, South East Queensland, Australia found that they lay up to 2052 eggs each. The eggs of phasmids are often dropped or flicked to the ground (as in *titan*), buried, glued in crevices or on to branches or leaves, or sometimes pierced in leaves. The knob present on the lid of some eggs may attract ants, who take the eggs underground and then eat the knobs (as reported in Australia and South Africa). The eggs, protected from parasites and ground-dwelling predators, eventually hatch and the emerging nymphs push to the surface.

Eurycnema goliath female from Queensland Australia – defence display.

6 In self defence, a phasmid may suddenly open bright wings, hiss, or kick out at a potential predator with spiny hind legs. Some species remain motionless (possibly after dropping to the ground, where they appear to vanish), emit a fluid from their mouthparts or spray an irritating chemical a distance of up to 20cm (8in). In a few extreme cases, this has caused temporary blindness in humans.

7 Phasmids often, though not always, breed by parthenogenesis – that is, females lay eggs, which develop without fertilisation, hatching into females only. It is a way of continuing the species when males are not available.

8 Autotomy is a useful feature in phasmids and involves the shedding or breaking off of a damaged limb (perhaps one discarded in an attempt to flee a predator) at a specialised point where the leg joins the body, with subsequent regeneration

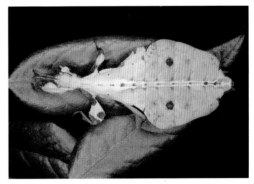

A male Javan Leaf Insect re-growing the fore- and midlegs on its right side.

during moults. Only nymphs (the young of the species) have the ability to regenerate lost limbs and antennae; regrown legs are usually shorter than the original, but will be nearer the size of a normal adult leg if regeneration starts at an early nymphal stage.

9   Phasmids just fall outside the 10 most popular pets in the United Kingdom, and more than 100 species of phasmid are being cultured by enthusiasts in Europe alone. The Laboratory or Indian Stick Insect (*Carausius morosus*) is kept by many schools and is easily available. Hundreds of papers have been published relating to studies of this single species.

10   Groups dedicated to phasmids include the United Kingdom based Phasmid Study Group (founded in 1980), with a world-wide membership of over 500 professional and amateur enthusiasts. It publishes a newsletter and journal and members exchange livestock, subject to a key rule that stock obtained through the Group must not be sold by members. Smaller European organisations also publish information in their own languages.

11   Although phasmids are often not noticed because they are mainly nocturnal (active at night), some species occur in 'pest' numbers. These include the Spurlegged Phasmatid (*Didymuria violescens*) from Australia, which caused spectacular damage to mountain areas of New South Wales and Victoria in 1963, defoliating 650 square miles of Eucalyptus forest. In the 1800s there were reports of the Coconut Stick Insect (*Graeffea crouanii*) from the South Sea Isles contributing to cannibalism in some of the islands 'due to the want of food caused by the ravages of these insects [on coconut leaves]'.

12   Adults of some phasmids, for example species of the South-East Asian genera *Dares* and *Pylaemenes*, commonly live for 2–3 years, although most species die several months after reaching the adult stage.

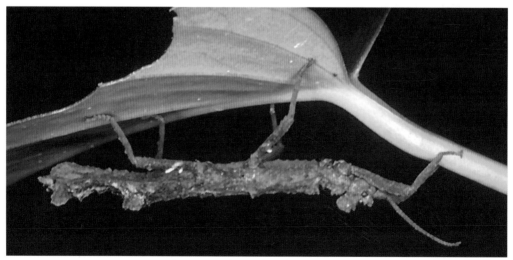

Pylaemenes mitratus **female, Singapore.**

two

Basic Requirements

Cage and foodplant.

The following is intended as an indication of minimum requirements before going ahead and purchasing or obtaining phasmids as pets. Please refer to Chapter 4 (Housing) and Chapter 5 (Feeding) for more detailed information about the options available.

- A tall, well ventilated, spacious cage. If you do not have access to larger cages, you should only keep smaller species. Those on low budgets could even adapt large jam or sweet jars.

- A jam jar or similar container to insert the foodplant branches.

- Newspaper or another lining for the bottom of the cage.

- Suitable small plastic containers for keeping and hatching eggs. The eggs can be laid out on surfaces such as slightly moist sand or tissue paper.

- Sufficient temperature and humidity for the insects being reared. Artificial heating may be required.

- A sufficient and regular supply of foodplant. Bramble or blackberry bush (*Rubus fruticosus*) leaves are preferred by many species, so a pair of secateurs or strong scissors and gardening gloves are useful to protect against sharp thorns on the branches and stems.

- Sufficient time to look after the insects. They need to be cleaned out at least once a week, more often if the foodplant leaves are starting to wilt. Daily checks of eggs are needed, with a view to transferring the newly-hatched nymphs to another container, with foodplant.

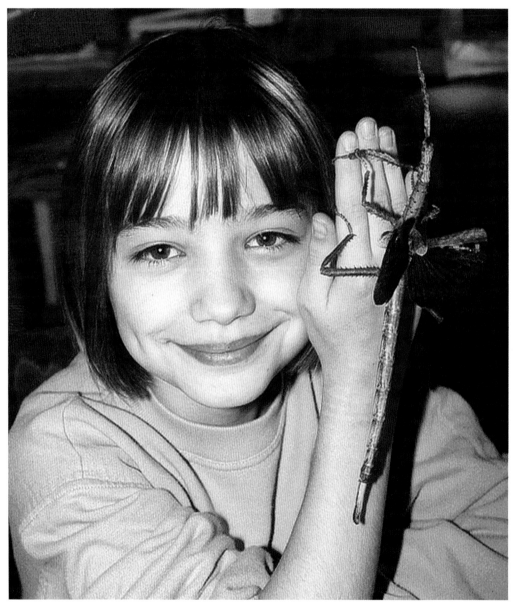

A delighted youngster handling an *Achrioptera* species female from Madagascar.

How to Obtain Live Phasmids *three*

A butterfly house in Penang, Malaysia. The giant leaf insect sign shows the way!

Spot the phasmid! A Malayan butterfly house.

Enthusiasts may wish to join a specialist organisation such as the Phasmid Study Group (see **Organisations**), where members have access to surplus stocks of many species (mainly eggs) at no cost. The main rule is that stock obtained through the Group must not be sold.

The other option is to purchase stock from suppliers, such as entomological (insect) dealers (who often stock several species of phasmids, in addition to other insects), pet shops, butterfly houses, or at entomological or general pet fairs. Details of fairs are given in the Newsletter of the Phasmid Study Group. Lists of dealers and contacts are published and periodically updated by the Amateur Entomologists' Society and Young Entomologists' Society (see **Organisations**). If pet shops do not have phasmids in stock, they can often obtain them.

I am often asked which stage is most suitable, or which species is 'best' to keep. The decision is entirely a matter of individual preference, but the following comments include feedback from first-time phasmid-keepers and may help you with your decision.

Which stage?

Some people prefer to start with eggs, to have the satisfaction of seeing the complete life cycle, but patience is needed as eggs often take several months to hatch. Most complete newcomers prefer to obtain adults or well established nymphs – those that have moulted a few times and are nearly adult. Buying adults can cause disappointment because some dealers sell specimens that do not have long to live, resulting in few or no eggs to continue the culture. Also, the insects might be kept by the purchaser in completely different

An insect fair in Paris. Fairs are held all over Europe, and sometimes further afield.

conditions from those to which they were accustomed, and they might fail to adapt. Always obtain pairs where both sexes are present in species; I have heard several stories of individuals buying females only of species such as Macleay's Spectre, and finding that the resulting eggs fail to hatch. Try to check that specimens are healthy. For instance, in a pet shop, make sure they have fresh leaves to feed on. I sometimes see the Indian Stick Insect kept in appalling conditions, with some dead and sickly looking insects in a container with only dried-up privet leaves.

Which species?

I tend to recommend a typical stick-like insect such as the Indian Stick Insect for the absolute beginner. This is a medium-sized species, easy to rear on privet leaves and remarkably hardy at normal room temperature. Success can be almost guaranteed and will provide the beginner with a sense of satisfaction. Children would be particularly disappointed to start with more difficult, although spectacular-looking, species which then died. It is preferable to gain experience before progressing to species such as Macleay's Spectre, the Jungle Nymph and the more difficult to rear leaf insects.

If you are interested in a specific species, read about it first to ensure that it is suitable for you to keep. For instance, do you have the right sized cage and access to the correct foodplant; do you want species with aggressive behaviour such as the Jungle Nymph; and can you keep the insects at high temperatures all year round if necessary? Some individuals derive great satisfaction from breeding the Indian Stick Insect for many years and rarely keep other pets. If you want to keep two or more species in the same cage, consider whether they are compatible. For instance, bulky, spiny species such as Macleay's Spectre, Jungle Nymph and Giant Spiny Stick Insects should be kept in separate cages, as they may cause damage to other, more fragile species. However, many species will peacefully live together in the same container, provided that they are not overcrowded.

Housing

four

A wide selection of cages and growing foodplants.

It is very important to consider the needs of insects being reared and to provide the most appropriate housing. Species from the tropics require high temperature, high humidity and relatively little ventilation in the chosen container compared with European species, which require well ventilated accommodation. Containers of various sizes are needed for eggs, nymphs and adults.

Many containers make suitable housing for phasmids, but frequently used examples include:

- Large jam or sweet jars with netting on top, tightly secured by an elastic band. Holes can be punched in the sides or lids of plastic jars if necessary.
- Fish-tanks or aquariums with ventilation holes in the lid, rather than standard aquarium hoods. Second-hand aquariums may be available. These are sometimes advertised in local papers or aquarian suppliers, which may stock tanks with well ventilated hoods for housing non-aquatic animals.
- Vivariums with heating equipment, most commonly used for reptiles and amphibians, are suitable for phasmids, although they are more expensive than aquariums.
- Cages sold by natural history dealers may include plastic, wooden or glass containers, with varying means of entry and degrees of ventilation. Some inexpensive, lightweight plastic cages are now available, with ventilation holes for jungle species or black nylon netting or gauze for insects from temperate regions, and these are ideal for many species. The cost varies, depending on the supplier and how elaborate the cages are.
- Plastic plant propagators with variable ventilation settings, the more expensive versions of which include a built-in heater pad in the base. These are often sold in garden centres.

- 'Small pet' cages from pet shops, which are plastic boxes with ventilated lids. If you think the occupants may be able to escape through gaps in the lids, you can place a piece of fine black netting on top of the plastic box, then replace the lid. These are used to house small animals and usually have a carrying handle for easy transportation.
- Some people prefer to make their own cages, perhaps using a wooden frame, plywood and black netting. However, there are so many alternatives on the market, including inexpensive options, that few individuals make containers themselves, unless they possess carpentry skills. In any case, I have seen some home-made cages that are unsuitable for some species.
- If you want a cage with flexibility, you could always use a net cage, with plastic sheeting outside the netting, to help provide humidity when rearing species that prefer such conditions.

A large cage housing Giant Malaysian Leaf Insect *(Phyllium giganteum)* nymphs on bramble.

In all cases, the container selected should have good visibility and be sufficiently tall for the insects being kept. The height of the accommodation must be at least three times the maximum length of the insects being reared. Plant propagators or aquariums may, therefore, need to be stood on end. Good access is also important – lift-off lids or doors on hinges are very efficient and make cleaning out much easier, although care should always be taken not to injure insects, for instance when sliding a door open. Glass cages (best with sliding doors) and aquariums tend to be heavy, which may be a disadvantage. Plenty of room is needed in the container, to allow the insects room to move around and moult; overcrowding must be avoided.

Having checked the caging options and costs you have decided what sort of container, but where will you keep it? Some people keep phasmids in the living room, kitchen, bedroom or study. Do not use insecticides in the room in which they are housed. Phasmids need to be reasonably warm, so try to keep them in a warm room. In temperate climates, phasmids should not be kept outdoors. Avoid keeping cages in direct sunlight or in a greenhouse, as extremes of temperature may kill phasmids. The widespread use of central heating in colder weather means that artificial heating is often unnecessary. If it is, you could consider heater pads or mats, usually kept beneath the containers. They come in a range of sizes and are very durable and reliable, providing an efficient heat source, except through glass or thick wooden bases. Pads can also be kept inside a cage. Inexpensive to operate, they can be left on all the time. Some pet keepers connect them to a reliable thermostat, which controls the heat output. These are included in some expensive propagators/cages. However, in normal circumstances, this is not necessary. Heating mats can also be used on the side of containers, although only 50% of the surface should be covered.

A temperature setting of 21–27°C (70–80°F) is suitable for most phasmids. I do not recommend using light bulbs, which have the disadvantage of drying up foodplants and can be dangerous; they might explode if they become moist, for instance as a result of spraying, and could represent a fire risk. If they must be used, ensure a hood is fitted around the bulb. Even where no heating is provided, an internal digital thermometer and humidity gauge are useful to monitor internal temperature and humidity both day and night. Many phasmids will not tolerate cold weather, although I heard about a recent case where a Pink-Winged Stick Insect was found on a doorstep one cold December, frozen stiff. After a few hours, the insect (which had been released in the garden a few months earlier) had defrosted enough to move around and feed.

The cage lining can consist of newspaper, which has the advantage of being absorbent. Alternatively, you could use tissue paper, white paper or similar. Ensure the sheet used is slightly larger than the container base, and avoid too many gaps at the edges, as smaller insects might become trapped in them. Some rearers use vermiculite (a growing medium for plants) for flooring.

Remember, different containers are needed for different stages, as described below.

Javan Leaf Insect eggs ready to hatch.

Eggs

Small clear plastic boxes are ideal. They are usually air-tight. Larger boxes can be used for keeping hundreds of eggs. Whilst these are suitable for some tropical species, ideally some ventilation is needed for many species. If you cannot obtain containers with at least some ventilation, you should cut a hole in the lid and tape netting securely over the top. The base of the container can be lined with 1cm of clean sand, which needs to be moistened by spraying water on it. After ensuring there are no puddles of water in the container, place the eggs on top of the sand. The eggs of species that bury eggs can be pushed into the sand. The operculum (lid at the top of the egg) should be kept upright. This has the advantage of visibility, in case

Tropidoderus childrenii **nymph from Queensland, Australia hatching from its egg.**

mould forms. To make sure you know which species are in each container, write details on a small sticky label and place it on the outside of the box. Spray the eggs once or twice a week, without soaking them. In some species from hot, dry climates, spraying triggers hatching.

Some breeders experience problems with mould because the eggs are kept too damp. You could try sprinkling a little methyl 4-hydroxybenzoate alongside eggs, which helps to inhibit mould. However, this chemical is expensive and may not be easy to obtain in some countries. If eggs become mouldy, you can clean them carefully with a small artist's or camel-hair paintbrush.

Besides a base of sand, breeders have varying success with alternatives, which include laying eggs on peat or tissue paper, again kept damp. The eggs can even be left in the main breeding container, suitable for species which glue eggs onto the container side; however, this makes cleaning out difficult and means that newly-hatched nymphs hatch into a large cage. Some rearers collect frass (droppings) and keep these alongside eggs in a container, to aid in keeping the eggs moist, although caution is needed as the eggs and frass may become mouldy.

Nymphs

Smaller containers are usually most suitable for small nymphs; as nymphs grow, larger containers can be provided. You can use either airtight plastic boxes for tropical species that require high humidity, plastic propagators or, where appropriate, ventilated cages.

Adults

Species from temperate regions such as Europe (including 3 species of stick insects established in the United Kingdom) and the United States of America must be kept in well ventilated containers; all-net circular hang-up cages are available from dealers in natural history equipment. To make them free-standing, wooden supports are usually available. Otherwise, large containers are appropriate, with less ventilated cages used for species from tropical countries.

Feeding

five

It is quite remarkable that tropical insects will often feed on bramble in captivity, regardless of their natural food, although some specialised feeders refuse it. All phasmids feed on leaves, although some also eat the flowers. For instance, *Timema chumash* from California, United States, become quite excited when *Ceanothus* flowers are placed in their container! Anyone who has bred a few species of stick insects will also know that some of them nibble at bark or eat the newspaper at the bottom of the container, which does them no harm. Always research which foodplant is suitable for the species you intend rearing and, if possible, give them a selection of leaves such as bramble and oak.

It is important to have a regular supply of leaves because of the appetite of most species, which often make large, circular bites out of the edges of leaves. As far as humans are concerned, bramble has the disadvantage of having prickly stems, so care should be taken in cutting branches – it is best to use gardening gloves and secateurs. This plant is often common in European woodlands, where it can be found all year round in sheltered localities. In winter, try to select the better quality leaves. This may be difficult in colder parts of Europe, particularly as hard frosts can kill bramble leaves. Where possible, trim off the brown edges of leaves and avoid collecting leaves from hedgerows close to roads. When cutting the branches, have in mind the size of cage you intend to use, although they can be cut shorter when they are put into the containers. If you cannot trace bramble in winter, check out alternative winter food, such as pyracantha and rhododendron, which have been successfully used in some countries with cold winters, including Finland. Some species accept a wide range of plants. Some phasmids dislike thorny plants, and they may sometimes become caught on a thorn, resulting in injuries, such as a wound on the body. However, they often survive. Even in spring, take care when feeding phasmids with soft, new leaves, which may contain poisons. Try to locate older leaves until the new leaves have hardened.

Macleay's Spectre female feeding.

Even a gynandromorph Jungle Nymph (part male, part female, with mainly male characteristics) can be aggressive.

You have a cage and suitable paper for the bottom of the cage, as discussed in the previous chapter. Now check the leaves you have obtained and remove objects such as snails, woodlice and spiders' eggs. Woodlice have been known to attack phasmids. Still using gloves, cut the branches to fit the container, allowing ample room for the insects to walk about. It is likely that several branches will be needed, which should be placed in a suitable size of empty jam jar, filled with water up to about three-quarters of its height. To avoid insects falling into the water, plug the gap with paper tissue or newspaper. It is possible to use a lid (preferably not metal, which can rust) with large holes punched in it to insert the branches. The leaves should stay fresh for about a week but, if you are using well ventilated cages, see the leaves starting to wilt, or have insects with large appetites, it will be necessary to clean them out more often by replacing the food with freshly cut branches. An alternative is to use growing plants. This is particularly useful if you are going on holiday.

Now for the task of transferring nymphs and adults to the container holding the new food: this might be a different cage, or the same one. If it is the same container, you need to remove the existing food by taking the jar out carefully. Do this in the daytime when the insects are not usually active and either use a table or have plenty of floor space available. Leave the insects and old food by the cage, remove the newspaper base and, if you have adults, put it on one side to collect eggs later; otherwise, dispose of it. If necessary, replace the newspaper after cleaning the cage out, and place the new jar containing the correct-sized branches in the cage. Make sure the jar is sturdy and cannot topple over. Then start to transfer the insects, which should have remained largely inactive. If you have quick-moving species that are active in the daytime, you need to place them in temporary quarters (for instance, another cage). Handle the insects with care, as pulling them could cause them to sustain a serious injury or shed legs. Do not pick them up by the legs or try to remove them forcibly from their perches. Most phasmids will walk slowly on to a hand placed in front of them, and can then be transferred on to the new foodplant. For larger nymphs or adults, gently pick up the insect by the thorax (avoiding the legs) after you have persuaded it to release a leaf or branch by touching the end of its leg, which will be resting on a surface.

Care should be taken with aggressive species, such as the Jungle Nymph, Macleay's Spectre and the Giant Spiny Stick Insect, although once regularly handled some individuals become less aggressive. Exercise even more care with species which release defensive sprays, such as the Florida Stick or Two-Striped Walkingstick (*Anisomorpha buprestoides*) from Florida, United States, as the spray may harm your eyes. If you are not confident about transferring nymphs and/or adults, or have hundreds of nymphs clustered on the old food leaves, use a sufficiently large cage and place a jar containing the fresh leaves alongside the old jar. This will save considerable time and the insects will gradually move on to the new leaves to feed, leaving the old jar to be removed subsequently. If possible, replace the water in the old jar; otherwise it may begin to smell. When discarding the old food, have a further look to ensure that you are not throwing insects away, as some are remarkably camouflaged.

As many nymphs and adults like to drink water droplets, spray the foodplant (with or without the insects on it) when cleaning them out, either daily or at least once a week. Purchase a plant sprayer for this purpose or, if you must use an existing sprayer, ensure that it has not been previously used with chemicals. Do not soak the leaves, because mould might form, which can be harmful to the insects; also, smaller nymphs might drown in water droplets. Leave the base of the cage dry. With practice, it takes very little time to clean out phasmids; most of the time is taken up in looking at them!

Always feed your phasmids. In the United Kingdom in 1994, the RSPCA instigated a successful case against a pet shop owner for mistreatment of stick insects, as the insects had not been provided with food or water.

Picking up the female of an undescribed winged species from Queensland, Australia, which readily displays its wings.

Successful Breeding

Six

Everyone wants to succeed in keeping pets, but sometimes enthusiasts are too demanding – they expect every single egg to hatch and every insect to survive and mature, which is not realistic. In the wild, of course, the chance of an insect surviving from an egg to reproducing adult is fairly slim, despite remarkable camouflage and elaborate defensive behaviour. Population explosions rarely happen because there are always predators to keep numbers down, so spectacular results can be achieved with captive bred stock, but rarely a 100% survival rate.

Children love to handle phasmids, although they may need to be supervised.

Sometimes success in breeding phasmids is achieved by trial and error. However, follow the basic rules given in the preceding sections on housing and feeding and you should not encounter difficulties. The trouble-shooter section which follows is designed to assist with typical problems, so the prospective pet-keeper should not be too concerned with these at the outset.

You now want not just to rear phasmids, but to breed them from one generation to the next. Some people become bored with keeping the same species, but others are fascinated by species such as the Indian Stick Insect and like to observe different behaviour in new generations. Surplus stocks can be given to those who want them or exchanged with fellow enthusiasts. Eggs are a convenient stage to exchange and are easily collected from the bottom of the container. Eggs vary in size, depending on the species.

Eggs are also the easiest stage to post, using a small, strong, non-breakable container in a padded envelope. Do not mail them in a normal envelope, or they will be crushed. Be careful when sending eggs abroad, as it is the responsibility of the senders and recipients of livestock to ensure they are complying with any laws regarding the shipping of livestock.

After removing the newspaper or similar from the container, either gently pick the eggs up

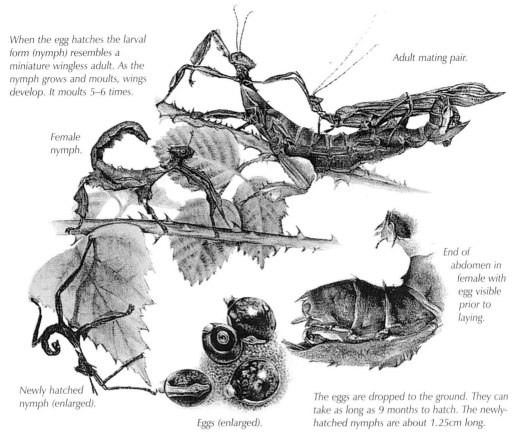

When the egg hatches the larval form (nymph) resembles a miniature wingless adult. As the nymph grows and moults, wings develop. It moults 5–6 times.

Adult mating pair.

Female nymph.

End of abdomen in female with egg visible prior to laying.

Newly hatched nymph (enlarged).

The eggs are dropped to the ground. They can take as long as 9 months to hatch. The newly-hatched nymphs are about 1.25cm long.

Eggs (enlarged).

The life cycle of Macleay's Spectre.

by hand, taking care not to damage them (they are very fragile), or tilt the newspaper slightly so that at least some of the eggs roll towards the corner where they are easier to collect. You can then transfer them to a small plastic box, with the help of a small paintbrush if necessary. Eggs glued on to leaves and branches, the container sides or the paper base need to be removed carefully with a slightly damp small artist's or camel-hair paintbrush, or you can cut around the leaf carefully. Eggs buried in peat need to be sorted out every week or so.

Try to keep track of the number of eggs you have, as this will help you to plan. Could you cope with thousands of Indian Stick Insects? Note that eggs take longer to hatch if they are kept cooler – keep them too cold and they will not hatch at all. However, some species from temperate climates actually over-winter in the egg stage. Incidentally, adult females lay eggs shortly after maturing, although some of the long-lived species that bury eggs may not commence laying eggs for about 2 months.

Females of *Paraclitumnus hispidulus* even glue eggs on each other's bodies and/or legs.

Newly-hatched Javan Leaf Insect.

If instructions about spraying eggs have been followed (in other words, once a week, or hardly at all for species whose natural habitat is dry, for instance those from Africa) you should soon see plenty of newly-hatched nymphs. These often hatch at night, pushing open a 'lid' (operculum) at the top of the eggs. In the wild, hatching in the dark probably affords them more protection against possible predators. Hatching will be helped if the eggs are kept warm such as in an airing cupboard, but not directly on a hot tank or radiator, as these are far too hot and will dry the eggs up. For the same reason, eggs should not be kept in the sun. The eggs of some North American and possibly other species from temperate climates, which undergo an over-wintering phase, can be subjected to a cold spell by placing the container of eggs in the fridge for a few months. The newly-hatched nymphs are often quite large for the size of the eggs and at this stage these often fragile-looking creatures, sometimes resembling miniature versions of the adults, need to be transferred to suitable living quarters. Take care! Some of these insects walk rapidly. For instance, watch the speed of the ant-like Macleay's Spectre nymphs, which could quickly vanish from sight. If you have a lot of newly-hatched nymphs there may be pandemonium when you open the lid. Most beginners gently coax nymphs towards their foodplant with a paintbrush, or let them walk on their hands and then transfer them. Do not pick them up with your fingers, as they are easily squashed, and the legs may be shed if nymphs believe they are in danger.

The newly-hatched (or first-instar) nymph is the most critical stage in breeding phasmids and this stage easily has the highest death rate in phasmids. They may have difficulty feeding. Perhaps the leaves are too hard. If this is the case, snip the edges of the leaves or introduce phasmids that are already feeding (have broken the leaf margins) as this may help the newcomers feed. Fast-moving nymphs may patrol the cages and apparently ignore foodplants in the first few days, but they usually settle down, start feeding and slow down. Do not be too disappointed when some of the nymphs die; think of how many hungry mouths there would be if they all survived.

First-instar nymphs grow larger as they feed, but in due course (2-4 weeks, perhaps), reach their maximum size and have to moult, or change their skins. This is achieved by the insect hanging from a twig or the side of the container for several hours to a day or more, before shedding its skin. The nymph is now much longer and this stage is known as the second-instar stage; likewise, a third-instar nymph has moulted twice, and so on, until the adult stage is reached. The moult involves a split appearing in a phasmid's skin along its back, just behind the head, and a laborious task of the insect pulling itself out of its old skin, which takes anything from 30 minutes to 2 hours. At this stage the body is very soft and the insect must not be disturbed, but must be allowed to harden. A spacious container hopefully allows the insect sufficient room to prevent it from being disturbed by other insects at this crucial time. If wings are present, they are expanded to reach full size. Before the adult stage, wing buds develop, gradually becoming larger at each moult. You may not see the shed skin, as it is often eaten as a first meal before the important task of eating leaves. Moulting is a delicate stage for phasmids and another area where things may go wrong, causing deaths.

Javan Leaf Insect nymph several days old. Has changed to green.

Most containers, including glass ones, are suitable for the insects to cling on to, but some, when moulting, may lose the 'claws' at the end of their legs that help them to climb up branches. Moulting is a precise function and occasionally things go wrong; rarely, an insect which has lost a leg may, for instance, grow an antenna in error! Other abnormalities can occur, but very rarely. For instance, insects sometimes hatch with 8 legs, or two abdomens, but these usually die very quickly. Gynandromorphs (part male, part female specimens) are sometimes reared, of which examples are illustrated in this book. Females sometimes lay abnormally shaped eggs, perhaps the first and last few eggs, although if they do hatch, nymphs are normal. Insects affected by conditions such as cold or extreme heat may make more or less moults than normal (usually by one).

Size variation within species can be significant. In captivity, the use of substitute foodplants may be a factor and sometimes (unusually) small specimens are reared.

Macleay's Spectre female moulting.

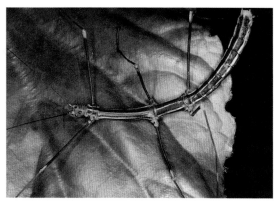

Gynandromorph of the Peruvian Fern Insect with mainly female characteristics, but reddish areas are typical of the male.

Close-up of the above insect.

Gynandromorph nymph of Jungle Nymph – half female (left) and half male (right).

Try to select the largest specimens for breeding. The effects of inbreeding (rearing species continuously without introducing new genes) can also have an impact. Where possible, mix fresh culture stocks into your own culture.

It is likely that the majority of species with both sexes present reproduce following the transfer of a spermatophore (sperm sac), more conspicuous in some species than in others and often seen on the floor of the cage. It is not known how many species are capable of breeding parthenogenetically in the absence of males. However, at least 6 of the 11 species covered in detail in this book can do so and my studies on culture stocks indicate that a figure approaching 50% is likely.

You would be very unlucky to experience problems with parasites, such as mites, parasitic flies or nematode worms, unless specimens have recently been collected abroad. Likewise, predators such as spiders, praying mantids, birds, frogs and lizards should not present any hazards to caged insects, unless they are being kept outdoors. However, beware of family pets taking a close interest in them. I used to have a helpful dog who kept an eye on any escaping phasmids I was cleaning out and became very efficient at directing them back into the container, using his nose! Some species with wings are very good at flying away as soon as a container is opened.

Each species has a different range of behaviour, of which the most common is feigning death by remaining motionless. Other examples of behaviour include swaying or rocking from side to side, and emitting fluids either from the mouthparts or from glands on the upper part of the thorax, which may be irritating to potential predators. Species with wings may open them and reveal bright colours in an attempt to startle potential predators. Spiny species may display aggressive behaviour.

Phasmids are sometimes observed cleaning their antennae, which are important in helping the insects detect their surroundings. If several species are kept in the same container, males of some species may become confused and attempt to mate with females of other species. It is very rare for these pairings to result in fertile eggs, although natural hybrids are known in the wild – for instance in Europe. Where there are a number of individuals of the same species in a cage, there may be competition amongst males trying to mate with a female, even where a male is already lodged on a female.

Finally, before departing on holiday, think of your insects and either make advance arrangements for someone to look after them or provide them with growing foodplants.

An important note on importing and/or releasing phasmids

When you are importing livestock, it is important to check regulations in your own country. In Britain consult *Plant Health Import Legislation. Guide for Importers: Importing Invertebrates* published by the Ministry of Agriculture, Fisheries and Food. Under current United Kingdom legislation, individuals may import any worldwide phasmids, but must not release them in the wild. To keep exotic phasmids in the United States of America it is necessary to have a permit from the United States Department of Agriculture.

What should you do with surplus stock? Some individuals exchange them with other enthusiasts, advertise them in local newspapers or give them away to schools that require them. If necessary, unwanted eggs may be destroyed (for example, in the freezer) to avoid being over-run with easy-to-rear species such as the Indian Stick Insect.

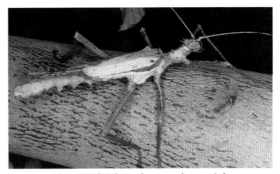

Gynandromorph of Jungle Nymph – mainly male, but green patches typical of female. Wings on right side shortened.

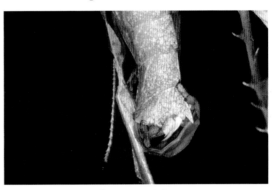

Mating in the Javan Leaf Insect.

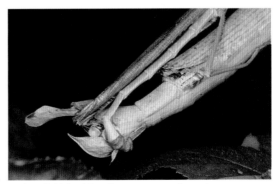

The pinkish object is a spermatophore (sperm sac) being transferred from male to female *Phasma gigas*.

A nematode worm, well over 20cm when uncurled, found in a 5cm Malayan species of stick insect.

This female *Haaniella grayii* from Sarawak displays brightly-coloured areas on underside.

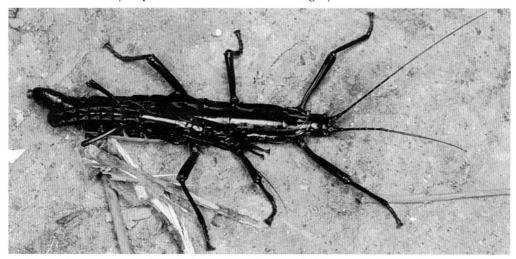

Anisomorpha monstrosa mating pair from Belize. They have bold warning colours and are also capable of emitting a foul smell.

Trouble-shooting

A number of problems commonly experienced by breeders are outlined below. The possible solutions given are only suggestions – not all nymphs will reach adult stage and sometimes they do die for no apparent reason.

Eggs fail to hatch

Eggs not fertile – they will not hatch. Ensure that males are available in bisexual species (although sometimes females lay fertile eggs if males are not available).
Eggs kept in incorrect conditions, for instance too dry. Spray them about once a week.
Eggs kept too cold. Keep them in warmer conditions.

Eggs parasited (more likely if collected in the wild), or attacked by mites. You may have to write them off and keep other eggs in another container, to avoid risk of an infection spreading.

Egg shell stuck to leg of hatched nymph
Carefully brush top of egg with wetted small paintbrush, allowing leg to pull free.

Nymphs stuck in eggshell and die
Eggs may be too dry; spray them weekly.

Eggs become mouldy
Clean eggs, using paintbrush. Sprinkle a mould inhibitor such as methyl 4-hydroxybenzoate near eggs. Consider using ventilated container, or reducing amount of spraying.

Nymphs fail to moult (insects caught in old skin)
Nymphs kept too dry. Spray regularly and consider transferring to different container. It may be possible to remove skin carefully, using a wetted paintbrush, a delicate operation which is not very often successful.

Nymph failed to moult (dead at bottom of cage)
Overcrowded conditions? Nymph may have been knocked to the ground by another insect. Consider placing nymphs close to moulting in separate cage.
Temperature or humidity levels correct – warm enough?

Newly-hatched nymphs have difficulty feeding, despite using known foodplants
Remove edges of leaves by cutting margins. Keep nymphs of other species in the same container, as they will break leaf margins. Fill box with leaves, so that insects bump into them.

Nymphs or adults suddenly die (not of old age in the case of adults) and are 'squashy'
Conditions incorrect? Too humid? Affected by mould? Overcrowding? Keep in drier conditions and thoroughly clean containers. Some breeders find tiny egg-like objects in droppings, which appear to be a mould and is often harmless, but following the earlier advice should eradicate infection.

Adults or nymphs weak – die for no apparent reason; not 'squashy'
Incorrect conditions? Too dry? Too cold? Are the insects lethargic? Too hot? Also, I have had apparently healthy females die when nearly adult, or having recently made the final moult. This may be related to using substitute foodplants in captivity. Wherever possible, provide a range of foodplants if you cannot obtain the natural foodplant.

Insects will not feed at all
Incorrect foodplants being used. If you cannot obtain the favoured leaves, try obtaining closely related plants from the same family.

Adults/nymphs appear disorientated and die within a few hours/days

Foodplants sprayed with insecticide? If you have bought plants, harmful chemicals could be in the system for several months and even washing leaves will not help. When purchasing foodplants, always ask whether insecticides have been used. Do not collect bramble or other leaves from the sides of roads.

Bodies bent/abnormally shaped

Likely overcrowded conditions, or cage not tall enough. Make appropriate changes. If the insect is rare and looks as if it may have difficulty feeding, it is possible to arrange a splint for adults with bent bodies (and perhaps nymphs). Pin the insect down under gauze (but not so that it is damaged – the pins should be crossed over legs and not enter any part of the body) and glue a matchstick, or similar, to the thorax (use Araldite) to straighten it. Leave for several hours and then release the insect. The matchstick should drop off after a few days. If used for nymphs, the support must be removed carefully; otherwise they will not be able to moult.

Legs drop off

Insects may lose legs on prickly foodplants when moulting, or shed them as a defence mechanism (the discarded leg may twitch for several seconds which might distract a potential predator). An adult will usually survive if it has at least 3–4 legs out of 6. However, it would struggle to survive if the 3 legs were all on one side of the body. Nymphs re-grow 'lost' legs, although the legs are smaller than in normal adults.

Adult females refuse to lay eggs

(They sometimes take 1-2 months before starting to lay.)
Does the species bury eggs? If so, provide small tubs of peat to facilitate this.

For species that glue eggs to branches and other surfaces (rather than dropping them to the ground), check these carefully before throwing the old foodplant away.

Adults considerably smaller than in previous generations

Possibly the effects of inbreeding (not introducing fresh stock), although in some cases such eggs might not hatch at all. Introduce fresh stock if possible and select the largest specimens for breeding.

Abnormally shaped eggs

Eggs occasionally abnormal, including the first few eggs when females mature and the last eggs laid before females die. These are unlikely to hatch.

Adults/nymphs appear sluggish

Kept too cold? Keep them warmer, heated if necessary.
Insects brought back from collecting trips abroad? They may be parasited by a nematode worm growing inside the body. You can do nothing about this.

seven

Structure

The structure of a stick insect is illustrated below. The body is divided into three distinct parts:

- head
- thorax (itself divided into three segments, the underside of each carrying a pair of legs; where present, the wings are attached to the thorax and are kept folded when at rest)
- abdomen (10 visible segments on the upperside. The hind segments are modified for mating and egg-laying)

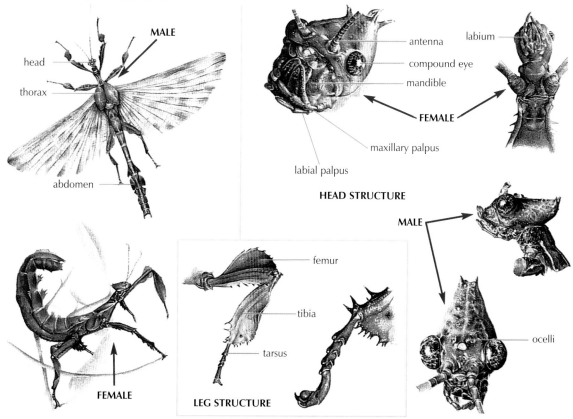

The head bears the sensory organs of the insect. There are a pair of compound eyes as well as ocelli (simple eyes), shown here on the male. The insect also has a pair of antennae covered with sensory hairs which help it to detect its surroundings. The male has longer antennae than the female.

29

The Species

eight

A rarity! A stick insect that feeds on the top surface of pine needles: the female of *Timema bartmani* (California, America)

The following 10 species of stick insects are the most frequently reared species. A leaf insect is also included, as many enthusiasts aspire to breeding these.

The common and scientific names are given for each species. The scientific name is in two parts – firstly the genus, second the species. It is followed by the surname of the author who first described it. Where the name of the genus has been changed, either by the same author or another, the original author's name is given in brackets. In all cases, measurements are given from the head to the end of abdomen. The overall length of the insects, including outstretched legs, is usually much longer.

The suggested temperatures are only a guide. If kept hotter, the insects may survive and certainly reproduce more quickly; they will usually be more active. Species kept colder may reproduce much more slowly and be rather lethargic.

Foodplants, including scientific names, are mainly from the following:

- bramble or blackberry (*Rubus fruticosus*) – common in Europe and should be found in sheltered woodlands all year round, except in very cold climates
- oak (*Quercus* species) – various oaks may be used, including evergreen varieties which usually have edible leaves in winter
- gums (*Eucalyptus* species) – although cider gum (*Eucalyptus gunnii*) is commonly kept in gardens in Europe, several other varieties are grown
- privet (*Ligustrum* species) – the species commonly kept in gardens is usually used
- guava (*Psidium guajava*) – often used in the tropics, but some keen enthusiasts in temperate climates grow them in greenhouses. Plants may be grown from seed or purchased from specialist garden centres

Alternatives used to a lesser extent include rose (*Rosa* species), raspberry (*Rubus idaeus*), hawthorn (*Crataegus monogyna*) and rhododendron.

Laboratory or Indian Stick Insect (*Carausius morosus* (Sinéty))

Culture history

The French physiologist Robert de Sinéty described this species in 1901 for the laboratory culture he was working on. Although he was using a 'manuscript' name *Dixippus morosus*, as advised by the well known scientist Karl Brunner von Wattenwyl, Sinéty is considered the author of the species, because he used the name *morosus* before Brunner's description in 1907.

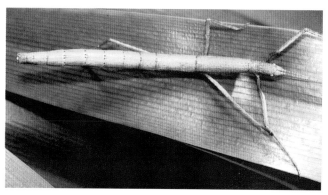

Indian Stick Insect female.

Although bisexual stock had initially been obtained from Shembaganur, Pulney [Palni] Hills, Tamil Nadu, Southern India (1830–2135m or 6000-7000ft), the males soon died out, leaving a parthenogenetic culture distributed widely throughout Europe. This culture has become very hardy and the subject of considerable research. However, males are still reared occasionally, perhaps one in a thousand specimens. Whether they are true males, capable of fertilising females, is questionable. It is possible that they are only gynandromorphs (individuals with male and female characteristics), for instance genetic females with male characteristics but sterile. These sometimes appear in cultures by subjecting freshly laid eggs to incubation at 30°C (86°F). This is the oldest established phasmid culture and is the species widespread in schools, making it by far the most kept phasmid 'pet'. I am not aware of any stocks obtained subsequently to specimens brought into culture in 1898.

Description

Stick-like, medium-sized, wingless insects with medium antennae, usually dull green or brown, in various shades and sometimes with darker mottling. In adult females the inside base of the leg is bright red. The thorax has a number of small tubercles (knobs). The thinner, shorter males are brown, sometimes with reddish markings on the thorax.

Length: male (rare) 48.5–61mm (2–2.5in), female 70–84mm (2.75–3in).

Life history and behaviour

This species is ideal to rear at room temperature without any special heating. This is not surprising, as they live at high altitude in the wild. Water droplets are appreciated by nymphs and adults. The eggs are round and brown with a yellow knob, and they hatch into fragile looking brown nymphs.

The following details are based on keeping the insects at about 70°F (21°C). Eggs hatch in 4–6 months and nymphs mature in 4–7 months, making 6 moults. Adults live 4–6 months, dropping several hundred eggs to the ground. Females usually start laying eggs about 2 weeks

Indian Stick Insect eggs.

after becoming adult. A cage with some ventilation is preferred, but they can be reared in almost any type of cage imaginable.

In terms of behaviour, this species is rather less exciting than others mentioned in this book. However, one cannot fail to marvel at the way they remain motionless for hours on end. Early researchers referred to the pencil-like attitude of these insects, with the front legs forward protecting the antennae and mid- and hindlegs held tightly to end beyond the abdomen, in a hypnotic trance, trauma or catalepsy, lasting up to five hours. This is a fairly extreme form of feigning death; normal activity can be stimulated by blowing on the insect, or gently touching the legs. When disturbed, nymphs and adults may sway from side to side; in the wild this could resemble a twig swaying in the wind. Specimens that drop to the ground use the claws on their legs to cling to a suitable surface, from which they may be seen to sway. Part of the defence reaction also includes discharging a fluid from the mouthparts.

The colour of these insects is affected by various factors, including food, light and foodplants. For instance, specimens fed on Forsythia and *Rhododendron flavum* become very yellow.

Foodplants
The most suitable foodplant is privet, often obtained from residential hedges, but a wide range of plants will be readily eaten. Ivy (*Hedera helix*) is sometimes used, particularly in winter, although it should be possible to find privet leaves all year round. Bramble may also be used, but with less success than privet. Other family members are sometimes astonished to see escaped insects feeding on houseplants. Escapees in the wild (perhaps deliberate releases or discarded pets) also feed on alternative foodplants if necessary, and the chain may survive for several years. Releasing non-indigenous species into the wild is illegal in the United Kingdom.

Distribution
Little is known about the distribution of this species. Brunner (1907) referred to various parts of India: Shembagonor and Trichinopoly in Madura province, with specimens in his own collection (Vienna, Austria) and that of Pantel (Paris, France). Well known French entomologists collected in the Palni Hills. Pantel's collection of *Carausius* species, including several other species he described in 1917, were caught by the likes of Dubreuil, Mallat and Décoly.

Escapees may turn up in various countries. Several years ago, I was sent adults found in the wild in San Francisco, California, United States of America for identification. I also recently found this species in the Cape Town area of South Africa. Specimens are believed either to have been released there or to be escapees from cultures kept in the 1930s.

Comments

This very prolific species is easy to rear and suitable for absolute beginners. I receive several letters and telephone calls each year: "What do I do with 'x' hundred nymphs or eggs?" This is a very good question! Surplus eggs are sometimes used as a welcome addition to the diet of goldfish, but eggs and nymphs can be exchanged with other enthusiasts, advertised in local newspapers or given away to schools who require them. As a last resort, unwanted eggs may be destroyed (for instance, in a freezer) to avoid being over-run with them. Keep them all and you must be prepared for a near-100% success rate.

Hundreds of papers have been written on this one species. For details of simple experiments, harmless to these insects, see *Rearing and Studying Stick and Leaf Insects* (1992), or try the following:

- Record colour variations/details of how long these insects take to mature when kept in varying conditions, including (1) different foodplants, (2) varying colour backgrounds in the containers used, (3) humidity and temperature variations, and (4) varying hours of daylight or darkness.
- Note details of behaviour exhibited.
- Keep records of how many eggs are laid by individual females on a daily/weekly basis and how long they take to hatch. Is the hatch rate better using different methods?

Etymology

Presumably the rather plain appearance of this insect prompted Brunner to select the Latin word *morosus*, meaning gloomy.

Mediterranean Stick Insect (*Bacillus rossius* (Rossi))

Culture history

Stocks have been bred in Europe for many years, mainly breeding parthenogenetically, although some researchers have kept bisexual stocks in the laboratory. The first specimens sold commercially were most probably from Corsica; hence the common name of 'Corsican Stick Insect' which, for many years, was wrongly identified as a similar European species, *Clonopsis gallica*, which is also cultured. The Mediterranean Stick Insect is a much more appropriate common name for a widespread species with culture stocks originating from several countries including Corsica, Croatia, France, Greece, Italy and Spain, particularly in the 1970s and 1980s. Often these stocks have been collected by residents or individuals visiting countries on holiday. Some laboratory studies on this species were made in France and Germany in the late 1800s.

Description

Stick-like, medium-sized, wingless insects with short antennae. Females occur in various shades of green and brown and have a smooth or weakly granulated thorax (small 'knobs' clearly visible with a hand lens). In adult females the inner base of the leg is red, or sometimes yellowish. There is a white (or sometimes red) stripe along each side of the body. Males, which occur in some colonies but rarely in culture, are brown and considerably thinner.
Length: male 52–79mm (2–3in), female 64–105mm (2.5–4in).

Mediterranean Stick Insect female.

Life history and behaviour

This species is fairly easy to rear in well ventilated cages at 20–24°C (68–75°F) and with humidity levels of 50–80%. About 2 weeks after becoming adult, females start to lay eggs. They drop over 1000 small, black, oval eggs, with a grey band, to the ground. Occasionally, up to 1500 eggs are laid. The eggs, which are sometimes mottled with greyish patterns, lie dormant for 3–8 months as these insects often over-winter in the egg stage. The emerging nymphs are green with short reddish antennae. Spraying the eggs with water may encourage them to hatch. Nymphs mature in 2–4 months and adults usually survive 3–7 months.

Where males are present, mating takes place for about an hour, although clasping of the abdomen can be maintained for about a day. Males can mate with different partners and, indeed, several times with the same partner. During mating, a spermatophore is transferred to the female.

When disturbed, nymphs curve their bodies, but the best defence these insects have is a remarkable camouflage, with an almost perfect match with branches or leaves, including colour. Whilst observing nymphs and adults in Croatia, I noticed that they gently swayed in the wind, like the branches.

In some countries (France, for instance) nymphs and adults are occasionally attacked by parasitic flies (*Thrixion halidayanum*). The fly larvae (grubs) are visible as small black lumps sticking out through the insect body. One or several larvae may live in a single phasmid until they have finished feeding. The cycle begins with flies looking for hosts, such as stick insects, on which to lay eggs. These hatch into grubs, which burrow into their bodies. The host is likely to be slow-growing during the attacks and may die as a direct result.

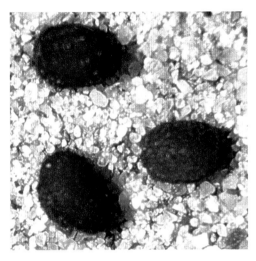

Mediterranean Stick Insect eggs.

Foodplants
Bramble is the most common host plant in the wild and the most suitable in captivity, although many species in the rose family (*Rosaceae*) will be accepted.

Distribution
Very widespread throughout Europe and the Mediterranean countries, particularly favouring coastal areas. It has been recorded from Albania, Algeria, Croatia, France (including Corsica), Greece (including Corfu and Zakynthos), Italy (including Sicily and Sardinia), Morocco, Spain (including Majorca and Menorca), Syria, Tunisia and Yugoslavia. Some populations are bisexual, but the majority reproduce parthenogenetically and are generally not found far away from the Mediterranean. Although they can be found all year round in some countries, the best time to locate them is between May and September. Occasionally, isolated colonies are found, such as one at Boulogne in northern France, which probably resulted from insects transported to the area from the south of France. When visiting any of the Mediterranean countries, look out for these insects on bramble and other bushes near the coast and in sheltered woodlands or meadows. Where exposed to extremely hot temperatures, such as on a bush by the coast, these insects remain well hidden in the daytime, but are easy to spot in the cooler evenings, when they start to move to the outer branches once again. I found good numbers of both sexes in the Rome area by searching on brambles in shady locations.

In favourable weather conditions, escapees from culture can become established in cooler countries such as Great Britain, although usually only for a year or two.

Comments
This is another prolific species, suitable for beginners. Most rearers who fail with this species treat them as tropical insects, keeping them at excessive temperatures or in cages which are not ventilated. Nymphs and adults are best not sprayed with water. The egg hatch rate is usually high, typically over 80%. If kept cool and dry over winter, eggs laid on moist sand and sprayed will begin to hatch. Eggs kept hot may produce more than one generation in a year.

Etymology
Named after the author, Rossi, the Italian entomologist who described this species in 1788 from specimens found in Pisa (Tuscany), Italy.

Pink-Winged or Madagascan Stick Insect (*Sipyloidea sipylus* (Westwood))

Culture history
Another culture that has been sold commercially for many years. The stock was collected in Madagascar by P Viette (France) in 1951. The well known French entomologist Chopard identified it as *Sipyloidea sipylus* and expressed surprise that this Asian species occurred in Madagascar. One can only conclude that the species was accidentally introduced to Madagascar from its native South-East Asia. The species breeds parthenogenetically; thinner 'males' are very rarely reared and appear to be sterile.

This is still a popular species to keep, and often the first winged stick insect reared by the newcomer to this hobby. Culture stocks are derived from the original importation.

Description
A stick-like species with medium-sized wings and antennae exceeding the length of its front legs. Females are various shades of brown or yellowish brown, either plain or mottled. In captivity most specimens tend to be buff-brown. The hindwings are whitish brown (almost transparent); buff-brown females have wings with a pink tinge. The rare male is like a more slender version of the female.

Length: female 83–88mm (3.25–3.5in). Reared males (not formally described) are about 50mm (2in).

Life history and behaviour
Another hardy species which prefers a humid atmosphere and may be kept at room temperature. A wide temperature range may be used (16–27°C or 61–80°F) with a humidity

Female Pink-Winged Stick Insect.

36

Female Pink-Winged Stick Insect with open wings.

of about 70%, although this is not essential. Nymphs and adults are fond of water droplets. Females glue a few hundred fairly long, brown, mottled eggs to various surfaces, such as leaves, in crevices or the side of the container. The eggs hatch in 3–4 months, with a high hatch rate, perhaps 90%. The newly hatched nymphs are green, about 19mm (0.4in) long and very quick-moving but somewhat fragile in appearance. They mature in 4–6 months, moulting 6 times. Adults live 6–9 months.

Pink-Winged Stick Insect eggs.

When you are rearing a number of this species, nymphs lie on top of each other in favoured parts of the container. When disturbed they secrete a fluid from their mouthparts. In an experiment, a secretion from glands on the thorax was shown to have an irritating effect on laboratory rats. Wings are sometimes opened when they are disturbed and kept open for at least a few seconds. Nymphs are very active when disturbed and sometimes get caught on thorny plants, shedding legs in the process. Nymphs and adults wave their antennae while moving around. Females usually manage a weak, fluttering downward flight, whereas males can fly well.

Foodplants

Numerous plants are accepted, but bramble is most commonly used. Some enthusiasts use oak, rhododendron, rose and others. This species will eat rose flowers in addition to leaves and suck the juice or nibble from apple slices. In the wild in Madagascar they feed on *Gossypium* and on various jungle plants in South-East Asia.

Distribution

I selected the type (original) locality for this species in 1995, based on a specimen from Java. During studies on these insects, I concluded that the species is also found with certainty in Madagascar, Peninsular Malaysia, Singapore, Sulawesi, Sumatra and Thailand. It has also been reported from Bangladesh, Borneo, China, India, Japan, Taiwan and Vietnam and has recently been observed in Mauritius. Most of these records are probably accurate, reflecting a remarkably wide distribution. However, historic records from Queensland, Australia are in error, as they represent a different species. Occasionally, this species has been found in the wild in Britain, usually following deliberate releases.

Comments

When designating the type locality for this species, I considered that males and females from India mentioned in the description were possibly of a different species, although a recent bisexual culture of the same insect from Sylhet, Bangladesh has remarkably similar eggs and may just be due to geographical variation. As *Sipyloidea sipylus* is a well known laboratory species, I decided that the Javan insect probably matched it, although I had some doubts following examination of Madagascan specimens in museums (often much darker than culture stocks). The position became clearer when I obtained a live female from the Tapah Hills, Peninsular Malaysia, which laid several eggs agreeing with the Madagascan culture stock. The colour differences in adults may be influenced by the insects feeding on a range of foodplants; there is no indication of a pink tinge to wings on the Madagascan wild-caught specimens I examined. This species is suitable for the beginner and can be very prolific.

Etymology

The name *sipylus* (derived from a Greek word) refers to the mountain in Lydia where, according to legend, Niobe was turned into stone.

Macleay's Spectre or the Giant Prickly Stick Insect (*Extatosoma tiaratum* (Macleay)) [Australian name: Spiny Leaf Insect]

Culture history

This strikingly unusual species was first introduced into culture in England in the 1960s, when entomological dealers started selling them. The species almost certainly originated from research cultures reared in Australia from North Queensland stock in the 1950s. It fast became one of the most popular phasmids in culture, sought after for displays by worldwide butterfly houses and zoos, in addition to demand from pet keepers. Although both sexes are present,

Female Macleay's Spectre, typical colour form.

females are occasionally capable of breeding parthenogenetically in the absence of males. Since the initial culture stocks, new stocks have been obtained from North Queensland and from near Brisbane, South-East Queensland, and these lay rather different eggs, although this may only be geographical variation.

Description
Males are brown, slender insects with black and white chequered wings. By contrast, females are large plump, spiny insects, remarkably heavy during their egg-laying prime (weighing in at around 20–30g, compared with only 3g in the male). They only have rudimentary wings, useless for flight. Usually buff or other shades of brown, they are often green in Australia, or sometimes yellow. This variation in colour may relate to foodplant variations or temperature/humidity differences. The legs and bodies of both sexes have leaf-like expansions. Antennae are about as long as the forelegs in the male, but are much smaller in the female. Males have 3 conspicuous ocelli (simple eyes) in addition to large compound eyes.

Length: male 75–115mm (3–4.5in), female 105–150mm (4–6in).

Female Macleay's Spectre.

Male Macleay's Spectre.

Life history and behaviour

The preferred temperature range is 18-25°C (64-77°F) and these insects may be kept in various conditions within this range. I recommend giving them a choice of at least two foodplants in a partially ventilated cage, sprayed once a week. Although some rearers succeed in breeding this species by keeping them in very humid conditions, heavy losses may result. The large, round, glossy eggs are catapulted to the ground and hence may travel some distance. They are mottled in various shades of brown, black and white. Two eggs are rarely exactly alike, but all have a wide cream band running the length of the egg.

The newly-hatched nymphs (18mm or 0.7in) are black with red heads. Their abdomens are curled around, and they run about at a frantic pace for a few days, before feeding. They may stop to feed on water droplets or attempt to nibble leaves. It is believed that they are afforded protection from possible predators by their resemblance to ants, both in colour and speed.

Eggs hatch in 5-8 months (hatch rate about 70%, or sometimes much higher), although parthenogenetic eggs may take well over a year to emerge. The newly-hatched nymphs mature in 3-6 months, with males moulting 5 times, females 6 times. Consequently, a male hatching on the same day as a female can be expected to mature about a month earlier. Males can be identified at an early stage by the development of wing buds. They also have much thinner bodies, lacking the spines apparent on female nymphs. Adults usually live several months, the females often well over 6 months. Males tend to die much more quickly and rarely live more than 5 months. In some Australian cultures, males live only 1-2 months and females 2-3 months. Females mate soon after becoming adult, although this often happens in darkness and you are more likely to see the 3mm white spermatophores (sperm sacs) on the container floor than to witness the mating. However, pairs sometimes remain mated for several hours the following day. Egg-laying starts about a month after females mature, and each female lays several hundred eggs, sometimes over 1000. An egg is often visible at the end of the abdomen, ready to be catapulted to the ground. This sometimes

Macleay's Spectre eggs.

happens when the insects are disturbed or handled. In captivity, thick branches are needed because adult females rest upside down with the abdomen curled, and are very heavy when fully laden with eggs. Nymphs and adults appreciate water droplets, particularly if they are kept in ventilated containers. However, some rearers prefer not to use a spray.

Eggs are best kept in a ventilated container and sprayed occasionally, which tends to trigger hatching. The newly hatched nymphs change colour once feeding begins. A sign that all is well is the red head darkening to brown. The body colour may lighten. After moulting, a wide range of colours may result, from cream to light and very dark brown. Sometimes very small specimens are reared, but these usually die much earlier than normal.

Defensive behaviour can be very elaborate and care is needed when handling adult females, as they have sharp spines on their hindlegs. The hindlegs can be used in a pincer action and, along with body spines, can cause minor bleeding to your finger. Nymphs and adults can lash out at an intruder with hindlegs and reach out and wave their forelegs. The abdomen is also curled around, which has been likened to a scorpion's attacking mode. Occasionally, clicking sounds may be heard during these manoeuvres. Defence glands in this species release a chemical causing a strong toffee-like smell, although this chemical is apparently harmless to man. This species can also sway from side to side.

Males can fly well, either a downward flight or sometimes upwards. In defence, they can open and beat their wings. Recent research in Australia indicates that females might attract the winged males by flashes of ultraviolet light.

Very occasionally, females will reproduce by parthenogenesis. The eggs take longer to emerge than normal, hatching into female offspring. However, the eggs of unmated females usually fail to hatch.

Foodplants

Bramble, oak and gums are the most commonly used foodplants in captivity. However, this species will accept numerous leaves from various families. Gums are included amongst their natural foodplants. Members of the public are sometimes startled to see such strange-looking, large insects in gardens.

Distribution

This species is fairly common in Australia in parts of New South Wales and Queensland, and has also been reported in Victoria and Tasmania. Whether all reports relate to this species is doubtful, due to variation in egg shape seen when comparing stock from North Queensland to that from South-East Queensland. It is unfortunate that the locality of the female *tiaratum* originally described was not given. However, cultures from different parts of Queensland may only represent geographical variation – research is on-going. Historic records of *tiaratum* from Papua New Guinea are of a related species *Extatosoma popa*, now in culture in Britain.

Comments

There are few more spectacular insects than females of this species. Handle them with care and you will have spectacular pets that are fairly easy to rear. Halved gynandromorphs (half male, half female) have been reported, although these are extremely rare.

Despite the Australian common name, this is not a true leaf insect, although it is easy to imagine why it was given this name, in view of the broad, leaf-like legs and expansions on the bodies.

Etymology

The Latin name *tiaratum*, means 'turbaned', relating to the tiara-like shape at the top of the head in this species.

Jungle Nymph (*Heteropteryx dilatata* (Parkinson))

Culture history

Originally imported from Malaysian entomological dealers in the early 1980s as eggs and adults, this spectacular species quickly became one of the most sought-after phasmids, helped by being on display in zoos and butterfly houses. The pet trade imported numerous adults, which were collected live in the Tapah Hills, Peninsular Malaysia, and transported to various countries. Fortunately, this trade diminished when this species was reared in good numbers in Europe. Dead specimens have been available from Malaysia for a number of years, where they are used for the insect framing industry (as a trophy for tourists) in addition to a demand from insect collectors.

Description

As with the previous species, males and females are rather different in appearance. Males are mottled dark brown, very spiny, with long wings that have a pale green or white margin. When exposed, the hind wings are bold pink, with dark brown veins. Females are often bright apple green on the upper surface with a dark green underside. Sometimes, they are mustard yellow with a green underside, or brown. Remarkably broad, spiny insects, the females have short pink hindwings hidden beneath large forewings (unsuitable for flight). A hardened ovipositor or lance-like structure at the end of the abdomen is used to push eggs into soil; females are very heavy when egg-laying (around 65g). Both sexes have long antennae.

Length: male 80–90mm (3–3.5in), female 145–160mm (5.7–6.3in).

What not to buy on holiday: a framed collection of insects, and scorpions, including the Giant Malaysian Leaf Insect *Phyllium giganteum*.

Life history and behaviour

These insects are best kept in humid conditions at around 21–27°C (70–80°F), so avoid using well ventilated cages. Higher temperatures may result in many more males than females. For small nymphs, I recommend a plastic plant propagator; leaves should be sprayed daily, but beware of mould. Nymphs are easy to rear and, whilst they are often plain brown (or green in later stages in the case of females), they may occur in several colour forms. As they grow, male nymphs lack the developing ovipositor or point at the end of the female's body. Instead they have a small bump underneath the end of the abdomen and develop wing buds much more quickly. Some male nymphs

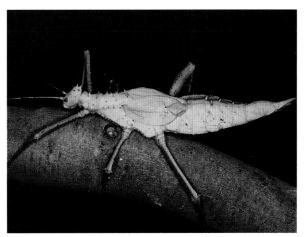

Jungle Nymph female, uncommon yellow variety.

develop bold white patches and/or longitudinal stripes, which are lost (or the stripes hidden by wings) when they moult for the final time. However, selective rearing of stock from colourful nymphs often produces successive generations with similar patterns, although this cannot be guaranteed. Larger nymphs and adults can be kept in large plastic propagators or cages suitable for jungle species (for example, plastic cages with several small, circular airholes drilled in each side). They need plenty of room so that they can walk around and make the final moult successfully. Moults are often made with the insects hanging by their back legs only. Females start laying eggs 2–3 months after maturing and require a tub of peat, sand, moss or similar in

Jungle Nymph female: (left) uncommon yellow and (right) typical green forms.

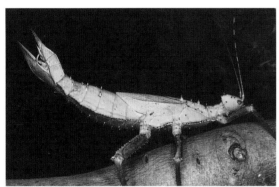

Jungle Nymph female (left) and pair (right) – the male is much smaller and browner with wings.

Jungle Nymph females, showing differing yellow and green forms, including nymphs (right).

which to bury the eggs. This container should be filled to a depth of, say, 5cm but at least 2cm. Sometimes eggs are laid in small batches.

The approximate life-cycle is as follows. A few hundred very large (up to 10mm long), oval brown or grey eggs are laid by each female, and these take 8–18 months to hatch (occasionally over 3 years). They must be kept slightly moist, but beware of mould forming around the lid of the egg. The eggs should be buried in moist sand or peat for hatching, with the lid upwards. Note that they change colour to almost black when sprayed regularly. When first reared, the hatch rate used to be only about 15%, but with care in removing infected, mouldy eggs, 40% or higher should be possible. The large, brown, newly-hatched nymphs moult 6 times (males) or 7 (females), taking 12–16 months to reach maturity. Adults usually live around 12 months.

The behaviour of *dilatata* is varied and extensive, particularly in the female. When disturbed she will typically cling tightly to a branch before arching her body forward with hindlegs extended, and these are very spiny. The fore- and hindwings are rubbed together, resulting in a hissing sound. If a potential predator, including a human, is still holding the

Jungle Nymph male nymph – left foreleg regrowing and wingbuds clearly visible.

insect, she will drive home the hindleg spines at speed, several times if necessary. This action can result in a painful wound. In extreme cases, she will also attempt to bite. Both these actions can draw blood.

The male has a similar defensive display, but lacks the hissing sound. Falling to the ground, he opens his wings, displaying bright colours, and has the same driving action with the spiny hindlegs. Males often fall on to their backs and pinch when you try to right them! Very occasionally, specimens have been seen biting off their own antenna, but more usually they spend some time carefully cleaning these.

Even small nymphs exhibit behaviour ranging from vibrating their antennae for several seconds to flopping around or falling to the ground and remaining motionless. The release of a fine, mist-like spray has also been observed, including in newly-hatched nymphs.

Gynandromorphs have been reared frequently, in addition to being found several times in the wild. These abnormal insects, in which some parts of the body show female characteristics while the remaining are male, are variable in this species. The most spectacular are halved gynandromorphs, left side brown (male), right side green (female) or vice versa, but these are less common than partial 'mosaic'-like gynandromorphs, which have the characteristics of one sex, with streaks of the opposite sex's colour (see pages 18, 24 and 25).

 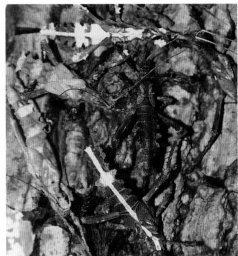

(Left) Jungle Nymph eggs and (right) colourful male nymphs.

Foodplants
Bramble is an ideal foodplant in captivity, although guava leaves are commonly used in South-East Asia and by some other breeders. In the wild they feed on various jungle plants including guava and *Rubus moluccanus*, a relative of bramble.

Distribution
This species is very common in parts of Peninsular Malaysia and is also recorded from Java, Sarawak, Sumatra and Thailand. It used to be found in Singapore, but is probably extinct on the island. In Malaysia, the Tapah Hills (Perak) area is the stronghold for this species; when rains come, they are reported to appear in numbers, drinking water droplets. While they are often found in hot, lowland areas, I have seen them at high altitude at Tanah Rata in the Cameron Highlands (Pahang).

Comments
A must for the more experienced phasmid breeder, who needs to be a little patient in view of the long life-cycle. You can be checking eggs every day for a long time before you see newly-hatched nymphs. However, you are unlikely to find a more spectacular insect to study or rear, or one with a more remarkable range of behaviour and colour variation in nymphs.

In Malaysia, these insects are sometimes reared by people for medicinal purposes - aided by the guava leaves the insects feed on. Chinese families believe that the droppings of these insects, mixed with herbs, cure many ailments such as asthma, stomach pains and diarrhoea. To cleanse the body, a brew is also made from the droppings, which are a concentrate of Vitamin E.

There are other interesting historical stories, including one from about 1900, when it was reported that rich men from the Kelantan region of Malaysia obtained the eggs of this species, which they considered a powerful charm against evil spirits, and set them in rings, like jewels.

Etymology
The Latin name *dilatata* relates to the expanded or broadened appearance of this phasmid.

Giant Spiny Stick Insect (*Eurycantha calcarata* (Lucas))
Culture history
First brought into culture by Allan Harman (United Kingdom), who collected specimens in the Kimbe area of New Britain, Papua New Guinea in 1978. Further stocks from other localities in Papua New Guinea have since been cultured and interbred with existing cultures. This is a very hardy species, popular in displays in zoos and butterfly houses as well as being kept as a pet.

Description
A dark brown, sometimes almost black, robust-looking, spiny species. Very occasionally, adults are green. The female has a large, beak-like ovipositor at the end of the abdomen. The male has powerfully built hindlegs, including large, spear-like spines on the underside of the femora.

Length: male 100–125mm (4–5in), female 120–150mm (4.7–6in).

Giant Spiny Stick Insect male.

Life history and behaviour
This species prefers warmer temperatures, but they are quite content at 18–25°C (64–77°F) with humidity of about 70%. Not only are water droplets appreciated by nymphs and adults, but they will drink from saucers, although care must be taken not to fill them too high. They may also be sprayed with water daily. They drink much more if kept in ventilated cages, although I have always found

Giant Spiny Stick Insect pair.

47

Giant Spiny Stick Insect nymphs.

large plastic propagators to be suitable, or alternatives with minimal ventilation holes. When you are cleaning them out they will drink water from a spoon. Eggs are best kept buried in sand, or similar. About 400 large, oval, light grey or brown eggs are buried by females. For this reason, a small tub or similar container should be provided at the bottom of the container, filled with about 4cm of peat or sand. Eggs hatch in 4–6 months and need to be kept fairly damp. If mould is avoided, the hatch rate can be satisfactory; otherwise it can be as little as 10–20%. However, the newly hatched nymphs (brown with a white patch near tip of antennae) are robust and nearly all should survive.

Nymphs take about 6 months to mature, often resting on top of each other. It is important to provide pieces of bark, moss, twigs, hollow cylinders or other objects for nymphs and adults to hide under. They moult 5–6 times, and are often mottled green and brown or buff, with a dark 'V' shape on the upper thorax. Adults live for a year or more, mating several weeks after becoming adult. The abdomen of the female fattens up considerably when she is egg laying.

Due to their aggressive behaviour, adults should be handled by placing your hand underneath; they will walk on to it themselves and will only attack if provoked. They are very aggressive and occasionally males attack and kill rivals. When disturbed they move their abdomens and the male emits a distinct, powerful chemical odour from the end of his abdomen. The hindlegs are raised and the spines brought together on a potential predator. If the 'predator' in question is your hand or finger, the insect may draw blood.

Although usually fairly sluggish, these insects can escape by walking away quickly. After about 3 moults, nymphs can curl their abdomens upwards or downwards. They can sway from side to side and are sometimes seen grooming their antennae. This involves bending an antenna towards the mouthparts, or just using the front legs.

Adult males are sometimes heard banging their abdomens on the side of the cage, perhaps establishing their territories. Males have been known to corner rivals and, during attacks, can lock legs. Even females have been observed to be aggressive with males, kicking out at them and sometimes causing them to retreat. However, they usually mate several times, with different males.

Foodplants
This species is easy to rear on bramble, and you can also use hawthorn, oak, rose and many other plants. In the wild, foodplants include coconut palms in New Ireland and croton (*Codiaeum variegatum*) in New Britain.

Distribution
Widespread throughout Papua New Guinea and surrounding islands, including New Britain, New Ireland and the Solomon Islands, where they are often found in numbers inside hollows in the bases of trees.

Comments
I recommend keeping this species separate from others, as the aggressive males have been known to attack and kill other species. They make delightful pets, but need to be handled carefully; particularly beware of the sharp spines. These insects are sometimes active in the daytime, although they are often in hiding.

Giant Spiny Stick Insect eggs.

Natives of Papua New Guinea have used hindlegs of a closely related species as fish hooks.

This species received considerable media attention in 1984, as a result of a member of the public finding an escaped (or deliberately released) female near Surbiton, England. It did not take long for the 'creepy-crawly' to be identified, following appearances on television and in the press.

Although learning behaviour does not extend to 'reading minds' or 'putting coins in the jukebox' and the insect certainly would not 'head straight for this guy's mug and start gulping down his beer' as reported in an American publication known for its exaggerated stories, specimens have been known to feed on pieces of apple left on top of their cage at about the same time daily.

Etymology
The bold spines on the hindlegs of these insects prompted the describer to name this species *calcarata*, Latin for 'spur'.

Peruvian Fern Insect (*Oreophoetes peruana* (Saussure))
Culture history
Collected from Tarapoto, Peru (valley of the Rio Shilcayo) in September 1984 by Didier Mottaz (Switzerland), this colourful species has been a delight to breed and quickly became a popular species in Europe.

Peruvian Fern Insect male.

Peruvian Fern Insect female.

Description

Males are slender and bright red, with black patches on their heads. Legs in both sexes are black with orange 'knees'. Females are colourful in a different way. They have a red or orange head with several black patches. The body is black with a series of yellowish stripes on the middle and sides. The central stripe is normally yellowish-green, the others yellowish-orange. The antennae are long in both sexes, black with a white mark before the tip.

Length: male 55–60mm (2–2.4in), female 60–70mm (2.4–2.8in).

Life history and behaviour

This species prefers warm (20–27°C or 68–80°F), humid conditions, and eggs need to be kept moist. Eggs are disc shaped and coloured brown with various black and grey markings. They are dropped to the ground by females and tend to darken before hatching, which only takes 2–3 months. The hatch rate is usually high and nymphs (12–15mm when newly-hatched, and black with a yellow head, end of abdomen and leg joints) take 4–6 months to mature. Some rearers have commented on high death rates when nymphs are young, but others have no difficulties at all. Adults usually live several months. Mating is sometimes observed and may take place for several hours.

Spray nymphs and adults with water daily and keep them in a plastic propagator, or similar closed container. They may be reasonably active in the daytime, walking around and waving behind them long antennae, which they groom regularly. Clean them out at least twice a week, as fern does not keep well, even in a jar of water.

The bright colours of these insects probably serve as warning colours in the wild, to help them to avoid being eaten by potential predators. Birds and other predators soon learn to leave distasteful insects well alone. They can eject a milky fluid from defence glands at the front of the thorax, which can irritate human skin if it is broken. Recent studies have shown that the fluid contains quinoline, similar to moth-balls.

Peruvian Fern Insect eggs.

Gynandromorphs (part male, part female) are occasionally reared in culture stocks (see page 24).

Foodplants
Although this is a fairly specialised fern-feeding species, it will accept numerous species of fern. Bracken can be found in sheltered woods in Europe all year round and is suitable, but should be supplemented with other ferns, either wild or cultivated. Take care when purchasing plants from nurseries or garden centres, as many plants will have been sprayed with insecticide or otherwise treated with chemicals that would kill phasmids.

Distribution
Peru and Ecuador.

Comments
An attractive, popular species that is fairly straightforward to rear and has spread due to commercial availability.

Etymology
Named after the country from which they were collected - Peru.

Touch Me Not Stick Insect (*Epidares nolimetangere* (de Haan))
Culture history
This common species has been collected by several people visiting Sarawak and has been in culture since 1988. Males from Mount Matang have much more green on the thorax and base of spines, although females are the same colour.

Touch Me Not Stick Insect: the female (larger insect) with two male colour forms.

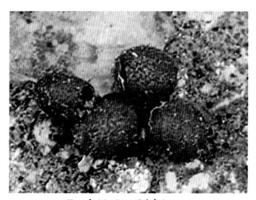

Touch Me Not Stick Insect eggs.

Description

A very spiny, robust-looking, small species with large spines on the head and thorax, variably coloured with black, dark and light brown. The antennae are slightly longer than the forelegs. The legs have just a few small spines. Females are heavily built and quite plump when egg-laying. Very rarely, specimens are reared without spines.

Length: male 33–39mm (1.3–1.5in), female 35–45mm (1.4–1.8in).

Life history and behaviour

A high percentage of eggs hatch in 4–5 months if the eggs are sprayed regularly. The brown newly-hatched nymphs are about 15mm long, with antennae a further 7mm. The abdomens are carried over their backs at this stage, and less frequently as they grow. It takes approximately a year for females to mature, perhaps slightly less for males. Adults are long-lived, perhaps living over 2 years, during which time females lay 1–2 relatively large, brown, hairy eggs a week. These sometimes stick to surfaces, including leaves, branches and the container side or base. Occasionally, a female has been observed to dig a hole, flick the egg over her head where it can catch on the antennae, then bury it.

This species should be kept in warm, humid conditions, such as in a plastic propagator. Nymphs and adults tend to hide, as they would in the wild, so should be provided with pieces of bark, or similar. The spines on this slow-moving species may deter possible predators in the wild. They can draw blood from humans if a hand is placed on them, as evidenced by one foolish collector in Sarawak!

Foodplants
Bramble, oak and numerous other plants. In the wild, various low-growing jungle plants.

Distribution
Fairly widespread in Borneo (Kalimantan, Sabah and Sarawak), sometimes occurring in good numbers.

Comments
This hardy species is easy to rear and requires little space. It has the advantage of being long-lived, so has become quite popular in culture.

Etymology
The species name translates from the Latin as 'do not touch me', an appropriate name for these spiny insects.

Guadeloupe Stick Insect (*Lamponius guerini* (Saussure))
Culture history
A pair of this species was collected from forest in Basse Terre, Capesterre, Guadeloupe in 1981, and further stock from Guadeloupe has since been introduced.

Description
Usually various shades of brown. Both sexes have a series of short spines at the back of their head, a pair of spines on the prothorax (upper part) and several blunt spines on the thorax. The male is slightly glossy. The antennae exceed the length of the forelegs. Legs are greenish brown, with some small spines; the inner margin of the forelegs is red. The female has very widened abdominal segments, although these vary in width and in some specimens are practically absent. Usually broad towards the seventh abdominal segment, and then narrow considerably towards the end of the body.

Length: male 65–82mm (2.5–3.2in), female 65–95mm (2.5–3.7in).

Life history and behaviour
Females live for 6 months, males a little less.

Pair of Guadeloupe Stick Insects.

Guadeloupe Stick Insect eggs.

The eggs are dark brown and cylindrical, hatching in 5–6 months into nymphs about 15mm long. The survival rate is high if they are kept in humid conditions. They often remain motionless and reach the adult stage in about 6 months.

Adults live for several months. Mating results in the transfer of a spermatophore (egg sac). The females lay several hundred eggs, dropping them to the ground.

Foodplants
Bramble, but will accept many other leaves, including oak and *Pyracantha*.

Distribution
Only found in Guadeloupe.

Comments
An exceptionally easy species to rear, this insect is now well spread amongst phasmid enthusiasts.

Etymology
Named after the collector, Guérin.

Thorny Stick Insect (*Aretaon asperrimus* (Redtenbacher))

Pair of Thorny Stick Insects. The male mounted on the female is not mating, but remains there to prevent other males from doing so.

Culture history
First cultured in England from specimens collected at Poring Hot Springs, Mount Kinabalu National Park, Sabah in 1992. Further stocks have since been imported.

Description
The male is much slenderer than the female, but still robust, being dark brown with a central beige stripe and side stripes of the same colour, which also features on the underside. Spines are present on the head and thorax in clusters in both sexes, and the body is generally granulated. The female is a plump, much drabber insect, and also has a few small spines on each abdominal segment. The ovipositor at the end of the body is used during egg-laying.
Length: male 47–58mm (1.8–2.3in), female 74–86mm (2.9–3.4in).

Thorny Stick Insect eggs.

Life history and behaviour
This species prefers humid conditions and has a reasonably quick life-cycle compared to close relatives. The large, cylindrical, dark brown eggs are laid in soil and hatch in 3–4 months. The brown nymphs have an excellent survival rate, reaching adulthood in about 6 months. Adults live for about 9 months and are sometimes seen paired up, but not necessarily mating. A spermatophore (sperm sac) is transferred during mating. You need to provide a tub of peat, or similar, for females to deposit eggs. They start laying eggs about a month after maturing.

When disturbed, insects walk quickly away or hide. It is therefore a good idea to provide them with bark or cardboard tubes. Adults emit a clear fluid from glands on the upper part of the thorax, which does not smell or cause irritation. Males sometimes exhibit aggressive behaviour towards rival males that try to mount the females. In the absence of males, females have been known to reproduce by parthenogenesis, the resulting eggs hatching into female offspring.

Foodplants
Bramble and oak are readily eaten, but this species will accept many alternatives.

Distribution
Common in Sabah, particularly Mount Kinabalu, its range extends to other parts of Borneo and Luzon in the Philippines.

Comments
This medium-sized species is easy to rear and therefore suitable for beginners.

Etymology
From the Latin for 'rough', or 'uneven', relating to the appearance of this insect.

Javan or Gray's Leaf Insect (*Phyllium bioculatum* (Gray))

Culture history

This species was first widely cultured from Javan stock supplied via entomological dealers in the 1960s, but has been imported and cultured from other areas since, including Malaysia, the Seychelles and Sri Lanka. Historical records include an 1850s record of a female on display at the Royal Botanic Garden, Edinburgh. The curator 'found it necessary, for the health of the insect itself, to forbid it being shown on more than four days in the week'!

Close-up of female Javan Leaf Insect.

Description

Both sexes have flat and broad, leaf-like bodies and legs with leaf-like expansions. Males are much slenderer and can fly well, as they have fully formed wings. By comparison, females have longer forewings and cannot fly. Often various shades of green, they may have brown markings, or vary in colour from yellow to brown. Females have very short antennae whilst these are much longer in the male.

Length: male 46–68mm (1.8–2.7in), female 67–94mm (2.6–3.7in).

Male Javan Leaf Insect.

Insect collectors start young in Malaysia!

Javan Leaf Insect eggs.

Life history and behaviour

A humid atmosphere is required, at least for the early stages, although some ventilation is necessary. Some rearers have recently claimed increased success resulting from using fans to promote air movement, but this is not essential. Some cultures of the Javan Leaf Insect are more difficult to rear than others and this may depend on the natural foodplant. After all, rearers are trying to ask nymphs to adapt to an alternative foodplant immediately. When they do hatch after 4–12 months (parthenogenetic stock takes much longer), try them in the following conditions:

- Temperatures around 75°F (24°C) and humidity of about 70%.
- Keep plenty of leaves in the container, so that they touch the sides and top of it. The newly-hatched nymphs are red (a likely warning colour to potential predators) and walk around quickly, so this method means they cannot avoid bumping into leaves.
- Do not at this stage spray the leaves, as the insects have been known to spend all their time seeking out water droplets, without feeding.

Two colour forms of the female Javan Leaf Insect.

- If the leaves are tough, for instance evergreen oak in winter, try keeping other phasmids in the container. These will break the leaf margins and may start the leaf insects feeding.
- Spray them during later nymphal stages, but beware of mould forming on the leaves. Leaf insects must have clean conditions at all times and should be cleaned out at least twice a week.

Good signs that leaf insects are feeding well are not only small black droppings on the bottom of the cage, but also the nymphs changing colour to green; they also slow down. Later on, nymphs need plenty of space in which to move around and moult successfully. The final moult involves considerable twisting and turning.

If you have sufficient nymphs, I recommend splitting them into at least two batches, with one kept cooler, to prolong their lifespan. This is because males sometimes live only a few weeks. For this reason, having matured before females (they make 5 moults to reach adult stage compared with 6 moults in the female), they may all be dead before the females mature. However, females sometimes breed parthenogenetically.

Mating involves the transfer of a spermatophore. Nymphs take several months to mature, and females usually live several months as adults, laying a few hundred eggs. However, if conditions are not to their liking, they die soon after moulting. The large seed-like eggs, quite unlike those of stick insects, vary in colour from light to dark brown. If the eggs are kept damp, the egg hatch rate is often high, perhaps over 80%.

Behaviour is mainly passive – these insects resemble leaves and do not have or need elaborate spines – but antennae stridulation can be used in defence by all stages.

Foodplants
Some cultures feed on bramble, but it is best to also provide oak and, if possible, guava. You could try myrtle, successfully used in Edinburgh in the mid 1850s, or *Nephelium lappaceum*, a foodplant in Malaysia.

Distribution
Widespread in South-East Asia; reported from Borneo, China, India (including Sri Lanka), Java, Peninsular Malaysia, Singapore and Sumatra. They are also found in the Seychelles and historically reported from Mauritius. There are old records of the poor inhabitants of the Seychelles rearing leaf insects and selling them as curiosities to sailors. They probably first reached the Seychelles on board a ship from South-East Asia. There are some doubts concerning the exact distribution of this species, which has not been helped by its wide variation in form – not only in colour, but also in body shape.

Comments
This popular species is one of several leaf insect species being cultured. Although they are generally more difficult to rear than many stick insects, some complete novices breed them with ease, whereas some experienced rearers fail time after time. However, they have not become 'as common an inmate of our conservatories as the canary bird now is of our dwellings', as predicted by one writer.

Etymology
The species name *bioculatum* refers to Latin for two 'eye-spots' on the abdomen of the male, described by Gray in 1832.

Other species
Many other species are available from every continent. These are sometimes offered by dealers, but more likely will be obtained through the Phasmid Study Group. Some of these species are illustrated in this publication. The above-mentioned Group publishes a useful list of species cultured by members, which is regularly added to and may be regarded as a guide to the likely species available. However, it is by no means exhaustive, as many enthusiasts and researchers rear other species in various countries. I estimate that about 200 species of phasmid are being cultured at present. Unfortunately, some species are 'lost' in culture almost as soon as they have been introduced.

Indian Stick Insect in the Cape Town suburbs, South Africa.

Mating pair of Thunberg's Stick Insect *(Macynia labiata)* on heather - Cape Town suburbs.

A flying female *Podacanthus viridiroseus*, a colourful eucalyptus feeder from Queensland, Australia.

(Left) Female Thunberg's Stick Insect *(Macynia labiata)*. (Right) Male Gray's Malaysian Twig *(Lonchodes brevipes)*.

A female Cape Stick Insect *Phalces longiscaphus* from the Cape Town suburbs, South Africa.

61

Organisations

Phasmid Study Group

Over 500 members in 30 countries, including individuals of all ages from beginners to professional entomologists. Exchange of livestock. *Newsletters* are issued quarterly and *Phasmid Studies* biannually. The publications will keep you informed about forthcoming insect fairs, meetings and the latest publications and topics of interest.

Contact: Paul D Brock (Membership Secretary), *Papillon*, 40 Thorndike Road, Slough, SL2 1SR, United Kingdom.

Phasma

A Dutch/Belgian group which produces a quarterly newsletter *Phasma*, published in Dutch.

Contact: c/o Kim D'Hulster, Rode Kruisstraat 36, B-9100 St. Niklaas, Belgium.

Amateur Entomologists' Society

Founded in 1935, the AES publishes a bi-monthly *Bulletin*, and a wide range of publications on entomology. The 'Bug Club' caters for younger members. Its annual insect exhibition is held in the vicinity of London and is regarded as the highlight of the year by many amateur entomologists.

Contact: AES, PO Box 8774, London, SW7 5ZG, United Kingdom.

Young Entomologists' Society

A long-established international entomology Society, which publishes *YES Quarterly* and offers many useful publications.

Contact: Young Entomologists' Society Inc, 6907 West Grand River Avenue, Lansing, MI 40906-9131, United States of America.

Further Reading

Alderton, D, *Your First Stick Insect*. TFH/Kingdom Books, Havant, 1997.
ISBN: 1 85279 170 5
36 pages. Suitable for the beginner, with a number of colour plates.

Brock, P D, *Rearing and Studying Stick and Leaf insects*. The Amateur Entomologist's Society, *The Amateur Entomologist* Vol 22, 1992.
ISBN 0 900054 54 9
Suitable for the beginner or more experienced phasmid enthusiast.

Brock, P D, *The Amazing World of Stick and Leaf insects*. The Amateur Entomologists' Society, 1999.
ISBN 0 9000054 63 8

168 pages+xvi and 40 pages of colour plates. A more advanced book, for those with a serious interest in phasmids and with a wide range of illustrations, including many colour plates. This publication is particularly useful for anyone who wants to collect phasmids abroad and/or keep a collection of dead specimens.

Schulten, D, *Wandelnde Blätter, Stab- und Gespenstschrecken*. Entomologische Mitteilungen aus dem Löbbecke-Museum and Aquazoo, Beiheft 3, Düsseldorf, 1995.
132 pages and 8 colour plates. (Text in German: a useful guide to breeding species.)

Index of scientific names

The principle references of the eleven species covered in detail in this book (including colour illustrations) are denoted in *italics*. Page numbers in bold face refer to additional colour illustrations of these / other species. *Note: common names have not been allocated to all species - these are given below, where appropriate.*